NATURE'S MYSTERIES

RAINBOWS

AND OTHER MARVELS OF LIGHT AND WATER

LYNNAE D. STEINBERG

Britannica Educational Publishing
IN ASSOCIATION WITH
ROSEN
EDUCATIONAL SERVICES

Published in 2017 by Britannica Educational Publishing (a trademark of Encyclopædia Britannica, Inc.) in association with The Rosen Publishing Group, Inc.
29 East 21st Street, New York, NY 10010

Distributed exclusively by Rosen Publishing.
To see additional Britannica Educational Publishing titles, go to rosenpublishing.com.

First Edition

Britannica Educational Publishing
J.E. Luebering: Executive Director, Core Editorial
Mary Rose McCudden: Editor, Britannica Student Encyclopedia

Rosen Publishing
Shalini Saxena: Editor
Nelson Sá: Art Director
Michael Moy: Designer
Cindy Reiman: Photography Manager
Sherri Jackson: Photo Researcher

Library of Congress Cataloging-in-Publication Data

Names: Steinberg, Lynnae D., 1957- author.
Title: Rainbows and other marvels of light and water / Lynnae Steinberg.
Description: First edition. | New York : Britannica Educational Publishing, in association with the Rosen Publishing Group, Inc., 2017. | "2017 | Series: Nature's mysteries | Audience: Grades 1 to 4.
Identifiers: LCCN 2015047013| ISBN 9781680484830 (library bound : alk. paper) | ISBN 9781680484915 (pbk. : alk. paper) | ISBN 9781680484601 (6-pack : alk. paper)
Subjects: LCSH: Rainbows—Juvenile literature. | Reflection (Optics)—Juvenile literature. | Color—Juvenile literature.
Classification: LCC QC976.R2 S74 2017 | DDC 551.56/7—dc23
LC record available at http://lccn.loc.gov/2015047013

Manufactured in the United States of America

Photo credits: Cover, p. 1 Anton Jankovoy/Moment Open/Getty Images; cover, p. 1 (cloudburst graphic) Macrovector/Shutterstock.com; p. 4 Kochneva Tetyana /Shutterstock.com; p. 5 Beau Wade/Shutterstock.com; p. 6 By Eve Livesey/Moment/Getty Images; pp. 7, 8, 10, 12, 13, 14, 15, 17 Encyclopædia Britannica, Inc.; Stieber/Shutterstock.com; p. 11 sebastianosecondi/iStock/Thinkstock; p. 16 Nina Leen/The LIFE Picture Collection/Getty Images; p. 18 Tischenko Irina/Shutterstoc .com; p. 19 Joanne Levesque/Moment Mobile/Getty Images; p. 20 Toshi Sasaki/Photographer's Choice/Getty Images; p. 21 Waddell Images/Shutterstock.com; p. 22 Martin Ruegner/Photographer's Choice/Getty Images; p. 23 Gareth Mccormack/Lonely Planet Images/Getty Images; p. 24 PhotoJanski/Shutterstock.com; p. 25 National Oceanic and Atmospheric Administration; p. 26 Doug Allan/Science Source; p. 27 Tomruen; p. 28 Pawel Papis/Shutterstock.com; p. 29 Hemant Me /Thinkstock; interior pages background patterns Eky Studio/Shutterstock.com (rays), zffoto/Shutterstock.com (waves); back cover, interior pages background imag Pavel Vakhrushev/Shutterstock.com.

CONTENTS

COLORS IN THE SKY 4
COLORS OF THE RAINBOW 6
HOW RAINBOWS FORM 8
THE WAVES AROUND US 10
COLORS AND THE COLOR SPECTRUM 14
HOW WE SEE LIGHT 16
NOT JUST RAINBOWS! 20
HALOS 22
OTHER WONDERS 24
THIS IS NOTHING NEW 28

GLOSSARY 30
FOR MORE INFORMATION 31
INDEX 32

COLORS IN THE SKY

A rainbow is a multicolored arc, or curved line, in the sky. Rainbows appear in the part of the sky opposite the Sun. They are usually seen in the early morning or late afternoon. A rainbow is really a full circle of light. Since most people view a rainbow while stand-ing on the ground,

The Sun must be at your back in order for you to view a rainbow.

VOCABULARY

Mythology is the collection of stories about the gods and heroes of a particular people.

however, they only see half of the circle of the rainbow in the sky.

People have been fascinated by rainbows for thousands of years. Many different groups have made up myths or stories about them. In Ireland it is said that there is a pot of gold at the end of every rainbow. In the **mythology** of northern Europe, a rainbow bridge connects the land of humans with Asgard, where the gods live. Many people see rainbows as a hopeful sign because they are often seen after a storm has passed.

Every time you move, your vision of the rainbow moves, too. You can never reach the end!

COLORS OF THE RAINBOW

Multiple rainbows follow the same curve as the primary rainbow below them.

The brightest and most common type of rainbow is called a **primary** bow. From outside to inside, the colors of a primary rainbow are red, orange, yellow, green, blue, indigo, and violet. A "double rainbow" is where a second, much fainter,

VOCABULARY

Primary means first to develop or most important.

arc can be seen outside of the primary arc. Very rarely it is possible to see up to four rainbows, but the last two are very faint.

The colors in the secondary bow appear in the opposite order of the colors in the primary bow. The dark, unlit sky between the first arc and the second arc is called Alexander's band. This area was named for Alexander of Aphrodisias, who first described it 1,800 years ago!

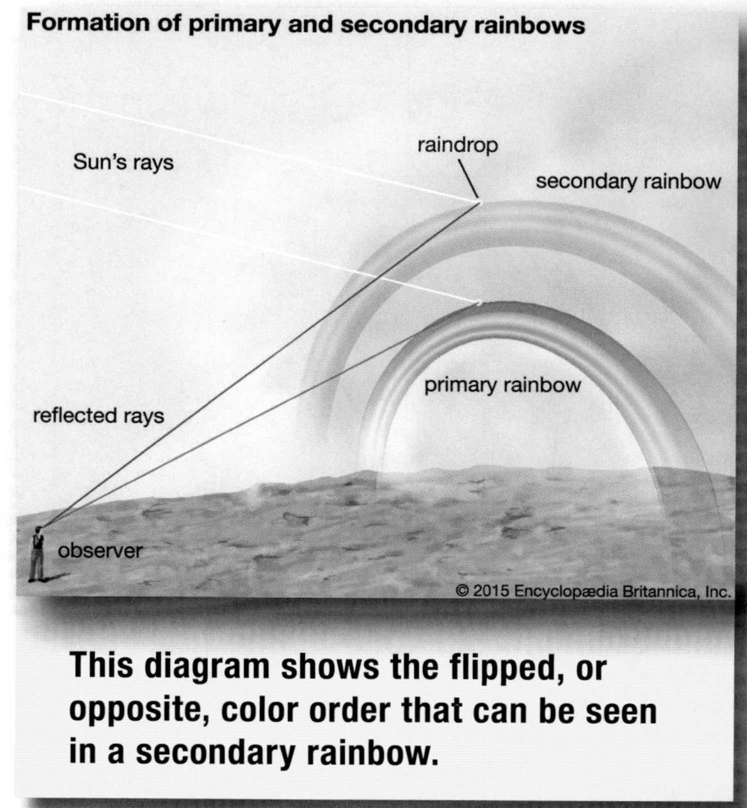

This diagram shows the flipped, or opposite, color order that can be seen in a secondary rainbow.

HOW RAINBOWS FORM

Most rainbows form when the Sun's rays strike drops of water in the air. Sunlight heats up water on Earth's surface. The heat causes the water to evaporate, or to turn into water vapor. This water vapor rises into the air. As the water vapor cools, it turns back into water, in the form of droplets. The droplets form

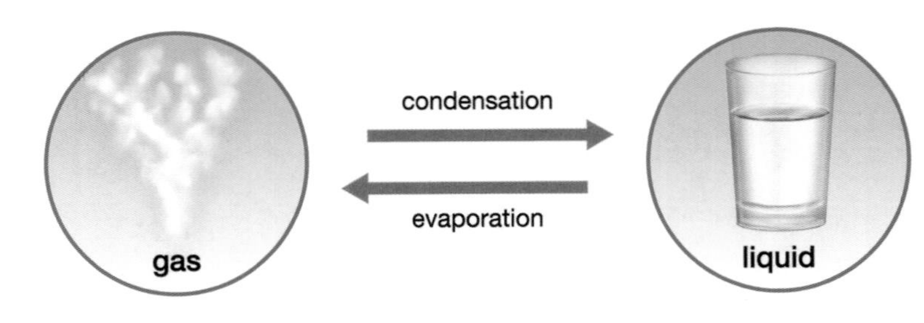

Evaporation and condensation play important roles in the development of rainbows.

THINK ABOUT IT

Why might a light wave be bent in a different way when passing through a water droplet than an ice crystal?

around dust and other particles through a process called condensation.

In a cloud, droplets come together to form larger drops of water. Eventually, the drops become too heavy and fall to Earth as rain.

When liquid water or water vapor becomes cold enough, it changes into solid water. This is ice. Ice crystals may fall to Earth when it is very cold. Light waves pass through the droplets or the ice crystals and bend, allowing us to see colors!

The water cycle never ends, so there is always a chance that rainbows can form.

THE WAVES AROUND US

You may only think of waves when you are at the beach, but waves do not only occur in water. Light acts in two very different ways. One way is as tiny particles called photons. The other way is as waves. Like waves moving across a pool of water, light waves have peaks and valleys. The distance between two of these peaks is called a wavelength.

Types of Electromagnetic Radiation

wavelength

radio	microwaves	infrared	visible light	ultraviolet	X-rays	gamma rays
used to broadcast radio and television	used in cooking, radar, telephone and other signals	transmits heat from sun, fires, radiators	makes things able to be seen	absorbed by the skin, used in fluorescent tubes	used to view inside of bodies and objects	used in medicine for killing cancer cells

Radio waves are longer in length while gamma rays are shorter than the waves of visible light that we can see.

THINK ABOUT IT

Why do you think the size of a droplet can affect how clearly the colors are seen?

The color of light depends on its wavelength.

Usually all light waves blend together to form white light. But when light waves pass through drops of water, the different waves separate. This happens because the drops bend every light wave of a different length by a different amount. The separated light waves appear as different colors. If light passes through larger droplets, the colors appear brighter, while smaller droplets create softer colors.

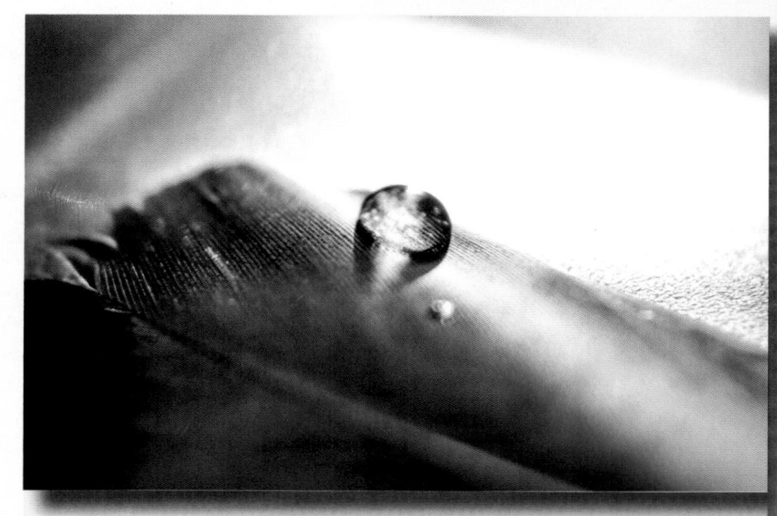

White light separates after passing through a raindrop, and the colors of the rainbow appear on this leaf.

White light also separates when it passes through a special piece of glass called a prism. Just as in a drop of water, when light travels through a prism, waves of different wavelengths bend by different amounts. Shorter wavelengths (violet, blue, and green) bend more than longer wavelengths (red, orange, and yellow).

Prisms may be found in binoculars, microscopes, and many other instruments. They help to bend the light that

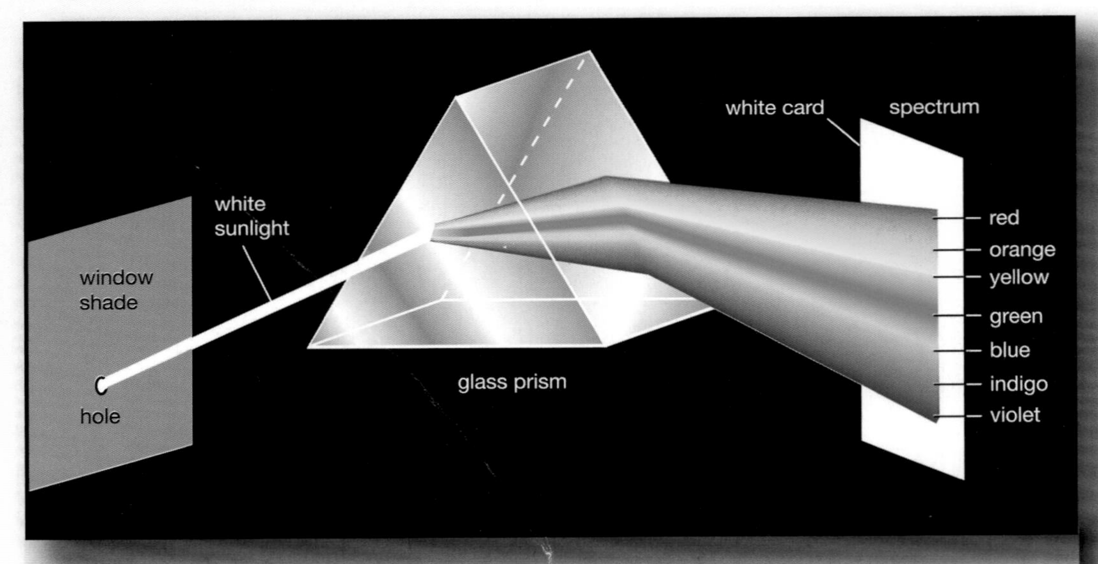

A prism, like a drop of water, allows us to see the colors that make up white light.

COMPARE AND CONTRAST

Compare water droplets and prisms. How are they alike? How do they differ?

enters these instruments toward the viewer's eyes. Light is one form of a kind of energy called radiation. Scientific instruments called spectroscopes act like prisms to separate other kinds of radiation. These help scientists study stars. Each chemical that makes up a star produces a different wavelength of radiation so scientists can measure the different wavelengths to tell what chemicals are in the stars.

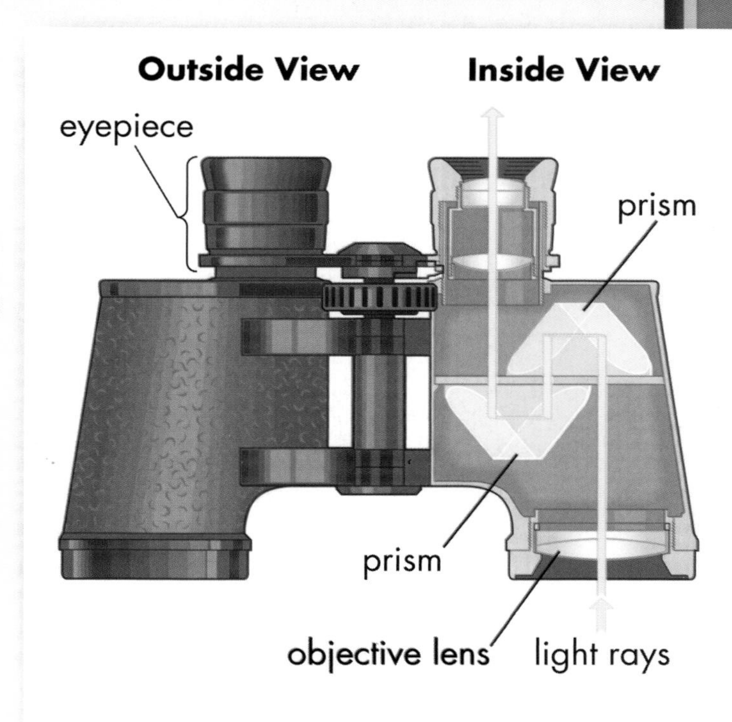

You can find prisms in various scientific tools. For example, they are an important part of binoculars.

COLORS AND THE COLOR SPECTRUM

Cells in the eyes called cones make it possible for humans to see color. Different types of cones absorb different colors. Three colors of light—red, blue, and green—can combine to make any other color. Because of this, red, blue, and green are called the primary colors of light.

In 1666 scientist Sir Isaac Newton identified the seven colors of the visible **spectrum** that together make up white

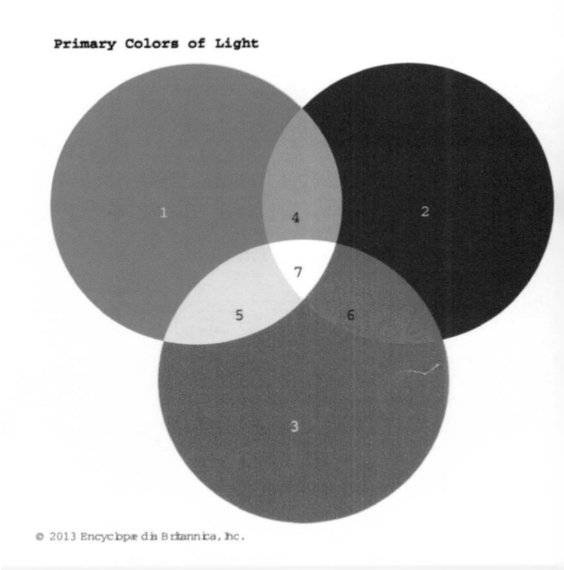

Mixing all three primary colors of light together will create white light.

VOCABULARY

A spectrum is the group of different colors that make up white light arranged in the order of their wavelengths.

light. All are present in a rainbow in the order red, orange, yellow, green, blue, indigo and violet. Many people use the name ROY G. BIV to help them remember the color order.

The color red has the longest wavelength and the color violet has the shortest. In a rainbow, the colors with the longer wavelengths are on the outside. The colors with the shorter wavelengths are seen on the inside of a rainbow.

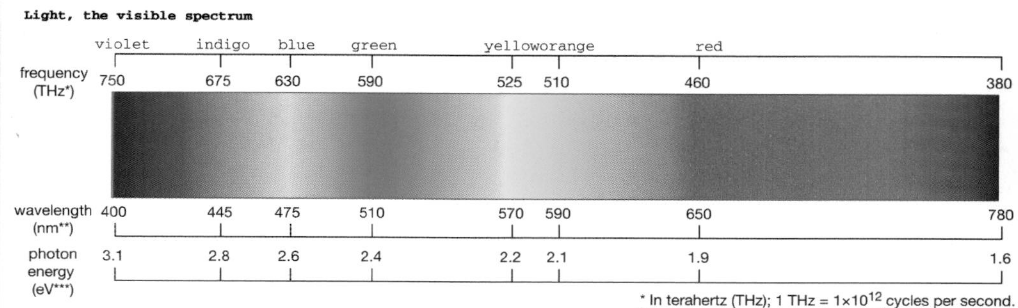

The order of the colors that make up the color spectrum can be remembered as ROY G. BIV, from right to left.

HOW WE SEE LIGHT

Light bends, or refracts, as it moves from air to a glass of water. When the light bends, the image changes.

Without light, there is no color. When people see colors, they are really seeing different types of light bouncing off objects. When light hits a surface, it may be refracted, reflected, or absorbed. Refraction happens when light changes direction, or bends, as it moves through one material to another. It is refraction that allows us to see the colors of the spectrum. Reflection occurs when light hits a surface and bounces back. Reflected light makes images appear

COMPARE AND CONTRAST

Try using a flashlight to compare how a sponge, a piece of aluminum foil, and a glass of water react to light. What do you think the light is doing when it hits each material?

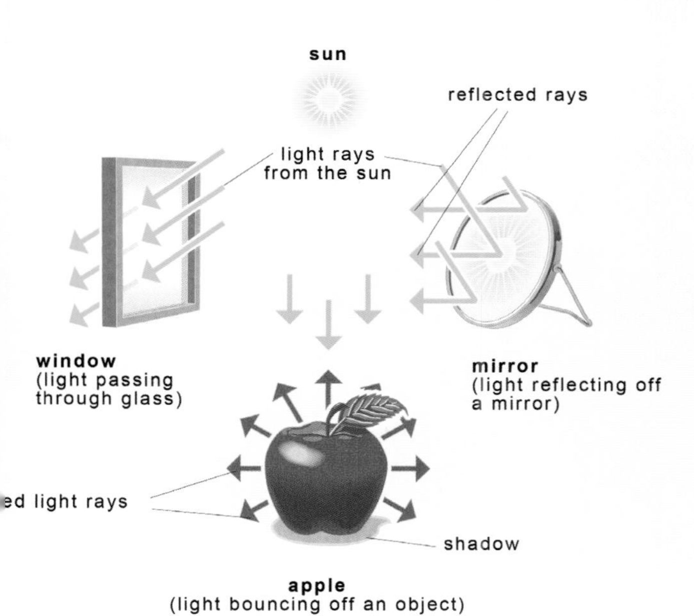

in mirrors and in other smooth, shiny surfaces.

A colored object reflects only certain wavelengths of light. The reflected light is the color the object appears to be. For example, certain apples reflect red light waves, which is why we see them as red.

A mirror reflects almost all of the light that hits it, while an apple only reflects back its own color.

VOCABULARY

To absorb means to take in, suck up, or swallow up something.

We can see through these drops because, like windows, they do not reflect or absorb much light.

Some surfaces don't reflect or refract light. They **absorb** light. This causes the surface to heat up. For example, a sidewalk heats up on a hot, sunny day because it is absorbing light. If an object does not reflect or absorb much light, the light passes through it. This type of object is called transparent, or see-through. Clean water, like a raindrop, is transparent.

Rainbows are created by both reflection and refraction of light in water droplets. No two people see the same rainbow. Even our individual eyes see slightly different rainbows. If someone appears to be standing under a rainbow you can see, they will see a different rainbow, at the same angle, but farther away.

Every rainbow is individual and unique to the person seeing it, even when two people are standing side by side in almost the same spot.

NOT JUST RAINBOWS!

This moonbow might also be called a lunar rainbow, or white rainbow.

Rainbows can also be seen in mist, spray, fog, and dew. A fogbow is formed by water droplets in cloud and fog. Fogbows are almost white with very faint colors visible. They are quite large and much wider than a rainbow. A moonbow is a rare night-time rainbow caused by light reflected from the

THINK ABOUT IT

If it's not really a rainbow, why might the fire rainbow be called one? Use the photo to guide you.

Moon. Our eyes see it as white even though all colors are faintly present. An icebow is formed through frozen ice crystals rather than water droplets.

One of the rarest sights is the fire rainbow. Fire rainbows are not truly rainbows, but they have similarities. They are also called circumhorizontal arcs (CHA). In order for CHAs to form, conditions must be just right. Fire rainbows can be seen when sunlight shines through a certain kind of cloud.

The rare beauty and power of a fire rainbow can be seen here through dark storm clouds.

HALOS

Halos are often seen as circles or arcs around the Moon or the Sun.

Halos appear more often in the winter months because ice crystals are needed to create them.

A special type of halo can only be seen when looking down from a high place like a plane or a mountaintop. It is

Unlike rainbows, halos may often be seen as complete, or near complete, circles in wintry skies.

VOCABULARY

A specter is a ghost. In the past, those who climbed the Brocken Mountains of Germany were scared to see a halo cast around a large shadow below them, and that led to its name.

called a Brocken **specter**, or a glory. It is a halo of colored rings that is visible on clouds below the observer. The person is actually seeing a large shadow of him- or herself with colored rings around the shadow. The colors follow the same order as a rainbow.

You must be looking downward from above to view Brocken specters, which makes sightings of them less common.

OTHER WONDERS

Sun dogs (also called parhelia or mock suns) appear as colored areas of light that are to the left and right sides of the Sun. They are formed when light passes through a thin cirrus cloud with **hexagonal** ice crystals. They are most often seen when the Sun is low. They look redder near the sun but may be green or blu-ish farther away. Moon dogs are formed by light reflected by the Moon.

It is easy to see why sun dogs are also labeled "mock suns." They give off bright light, similar to the Sun.

VOCABULARY

Something that is hexagonal has six angles and six sides.

A difference between sun dogs and halos is the way the light reacts with the ice crystals. If the crystals are vertical (up and down) when light passes through, the light waves bend more and colorful sun dogs may be created. If the crystals are horizontal (flatter, on their sides) the light waves may reflect more and may not be quite as colorful. Halos may be formed in that case.

How light reacts with ice crystals determines whether halos, sun dogs, or both (as in the image here) appear in the sky.

Columns of light, called light, solar, or sun pillars, are seen generally in very cold regions. They appear as cylinders of bright light extending from above or below a light source. Light pillars may occur when light reflects off flat ice crystals in the air close to Earth's surface.

Sun pillars are created by light reflecting off ice crystals close to Earth's surface so they may appear to grow right up from the ground!

COMPARE AND CONTRAST

Compare the color order found in coronas and sun dogs. Are they the same or different? Why might that be?

Another feature is called a corona. Coronas may be seen when looking at the Sun or the Moon through a thin cloud of water drops. Coronas look like a disc (circle) of light surrounding the Moon or Sun. A corona has a small number of rings with the colors in order from blue on the inside to red on the outside. Tangent arcs are also related to the reflection or refraction of light by ice crystals. Tangent arcs are similar to halos but have a “u” or cup shape in the sky.

Coronas around the Sun form when the edges of cloud droplets bend light a certain way.

THIS IS NOTHING NEW

Humans have been watching the skies throughout history. Before scientists learned what causes things like rainbows, ancient peoples had their own ideas about them. Ancient Greeks were known to use sun dogs to predict the weather. They knew that the conditions that caused sun dogs

Rainbows seem timeless, and people have watched them for centuries.

THINK ABOUT IT

Can you think of any other ways rainbows can be used to predict the weather or patterns in nature?

could also lead to rain. Native Americans of the Shoshone tribe thought of rainbows as large snakes that rubbed hail out of the sky.

You can find mention of rainbows and other related sights in stories and poems from long ago, as well. Greek philosopher Aristotle mentioned "mock suns" more than 2,000 years ago. Viewing a rainbow is to share in the wonder, beauty, and mystery of nature in our world!

People of all ages enjoy looking at colorful rainbows in the sky!

GLOSSARY

ANCIENT Relating to a period of time long past.

CELLS The tiny units that are the basic building blocks of living things and that carry on the basic functions of life either alone or in groups.

CIRRUS A thin white cloud usually made of tiny ice crystals.

CONDENSATION The cooling of a gas to a liquid state of matter.

CYLINDER A geometric shape composed of two parallel ends of identical size and shape (as circles) and a curved surface that connects the two ends, such as a paper towel tube.

EVAPORATE To change from a liquid state of matter into a gas or vapor state.

HAIL Small lumps of ice that sometimes fall from clouds during thunderstorms.

INDIGO A deep reddish blue.

INSTRUMENTS Tools or pieces of equipment used for certain tasks.

LUNAR Of, relating to, or resembling the Moon.

OPPOSITE Being at the other end, side, or corner.

SEPARATE To become divided or detached; to come apart.

SOURCE A point where something begins.

FOR MORE INFORMATION

Books

Beaton, Kathryn. *I See Rainbows*. Ann Arbor, MI: Cherry Lake Publishing, 2015.

DiSiena Laura Lyn, Hannah Eliot, and Pete Oswald. *Rainbows Never End: And Other Fun Fact*s. New York, NY: Little Simon, 2014.

Guilieri, Anne. *Rainbows.* Melbourne, Australia: Hinkler, 2013.

Rajczak, Kristen. *Rainbows*. New York, NY: Gareth Stevens Publishing, 2013.

Shand, Jennifer, and Daniele Fabbri. *Why Do Rainbows Have So Many Colors?* Franklin, TN: Flowerpot Press, 2015.

Whitfield, David. *Rainbows.* New York, NY: AV2 by Weigl, 2013

Websites

Because of the changing nature of Internet links, Rosen Publishing has developed an online list of websites related to the subject of this book. This site is updated regularly. Please use this link to access this list:

http://www.rosenlinks.com/NMY/rain

INDEX

absorption, 16, 18
Alexander's band, 7

Brocken specter, 23

colors, 6–7, 14–15, 16, 17, 21
condensation, 9
corona, 27

double rainbow, 6–7

fire rainbow, 21
fogbow, 20

halo, 22–23, 25

icebow, 21

light, how it's seen, 16–19
light pillar, 26
light wave, 10–12, 25

moonbow, 20–21
moon dog, 24
mythology, 5

Newton, Sir Isaac, 14

photon, 10
primary bow, 6, 7
prism, 12–13

radiation, 13
rainbows
  colors of, 6–7, 15
  explained, 4–5
  how they form, 8–9, 19
reflection, 16–17, 18, 19
refraction, 16, 19

secondary bow, 6–7
spectrum, 14–15, 16
Sun, 4, 8, 24
sun dog, 24–25, 28–29

water vapor, 8, 9
wavelength, 10–12, 13, 15, 17
white light, 11, 12, 14–15